JUPITER	SATURN	URANUS	NEPTUNE	PLUTO
483.4 million miles/ 778.3 million km	886.7 million miles/ 1,427 million km	1,783 million miles/ 2,870 million km	2,794 million miles/ 4,497 million km	3,666 million miles/ 5,900 million km
11.86 years	29.46 years	84 years	164.8 years	248 years
9 hours, 55 min	10 hours, 40 min	17 hours, 14 min	18 hours, 30 min (?)	6 days, 9 hours
88,734	74,977	32,000	30,540	1,430 (approximate)
hydrogen, helium	hydrogen, helium	helium, hydrogen, methane	hydrogen, helium, methane	very thin methane (?)
2.64	1.13	1.17	1.19	.08 (?)
16	21	15	8	1
1	1,000 (?)	11 (?)	4	0

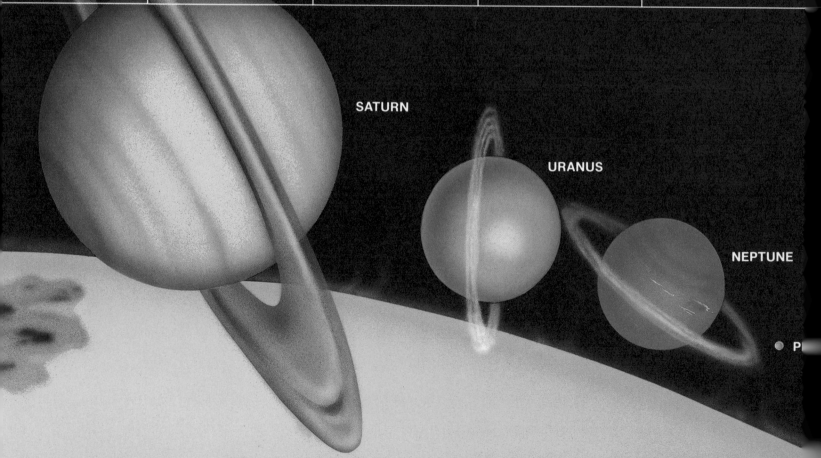

SATURN

URANUS

NEPTUNE

P

OUR SOLAR SYSTEM

SEYMOUR SIMON

MORROW JUNIOR BOOKS
New York

PICTURE CREDITS
Stephen Jay; courtesy Dennis Milon, page 62;
Jet Propulsion Laboratory, 13, 14, 16, 21, 32, 35, 48, 51,
52, 54, and 55; and
National Optical Astronomy Observatories, page 63.
All other photographs courtesy of NASA.
Original illustrations on the endpapers and pages 6–7,
17, 18, 24, and 58 by Ann Neumann.

The text type is 18 point ITC Garamond Book.

Printed in Mexico

3   4   5   6   7   8   9   10

Library of Congress Cataloging-in-Publication Data
Simon, Seymour.
Our solar system / Seymour Simon.
p.   cm.
Summary: Describes the origins and characteristics of the
sun, planets, moons, asteroids, meteoroids, and comets.
ISBN 0-688-09992-0—ISBN 0-688-09993-9 (library)
1. Solar system—Juvenile literature.   2. Planets—
Juvenile literature.   [1. Solar system.   2. Planets.]   I. Title.
QB501.3.S63   1992
523.2—dc20   91-36665   CIP   AC

For a moment of night we have a glimpse of ourselves and of our world islanded in its stream of stars… voyaging between horizons across the eternal seas of space and time.

—Henry Beston
The Outermost House

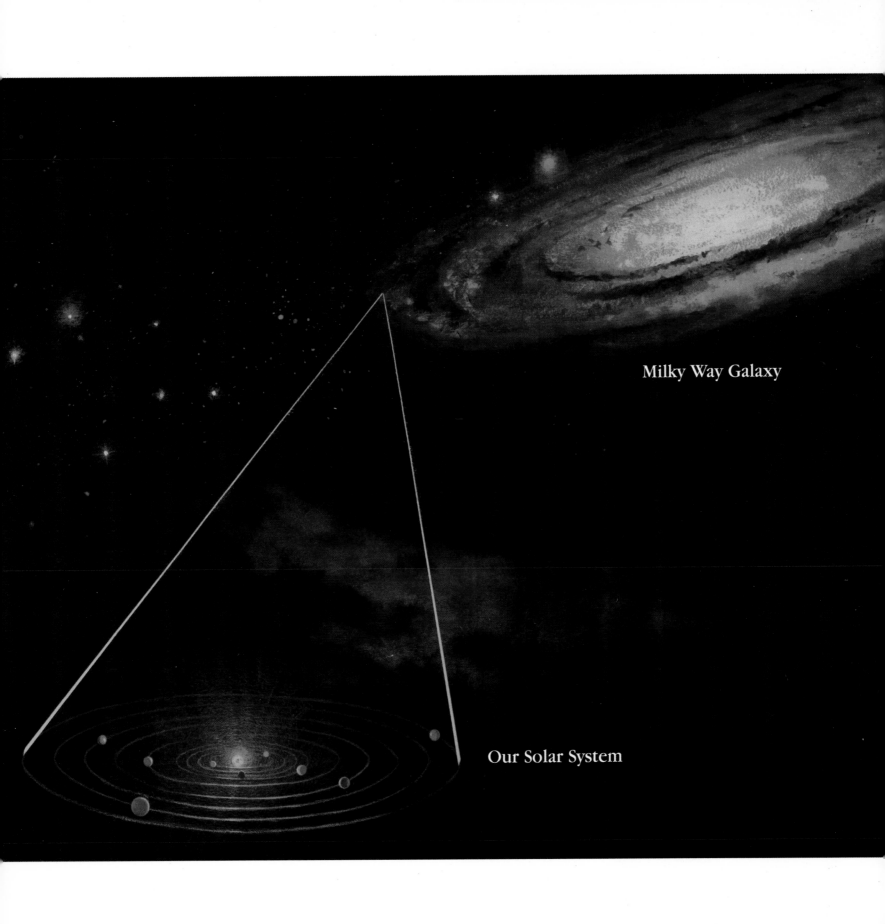

Milky Way Galaxy

Our Solar System

The Solar System was born among the billions of stars in the Milky Way galaxy. About 4.6 billion years ago, a huge cloud of dust and hydrogen gas floating at the edges of the galaxy began to pull together to form a globe. The particles packed more and more tightly together and became hotter and hotter. Finally the enormous heat in the center of the globe set off a chain of nuclear explosions, and the sun began to shine.

The blazing sun blasted away the nearby gases and dust into a spinning oval ring. As the particles in the ring began to cool, they clumped together into rocky or icy masses called planetesimals. These became the rest of the Solar System: planets, moons, asteroids, meteoroids, and comets.

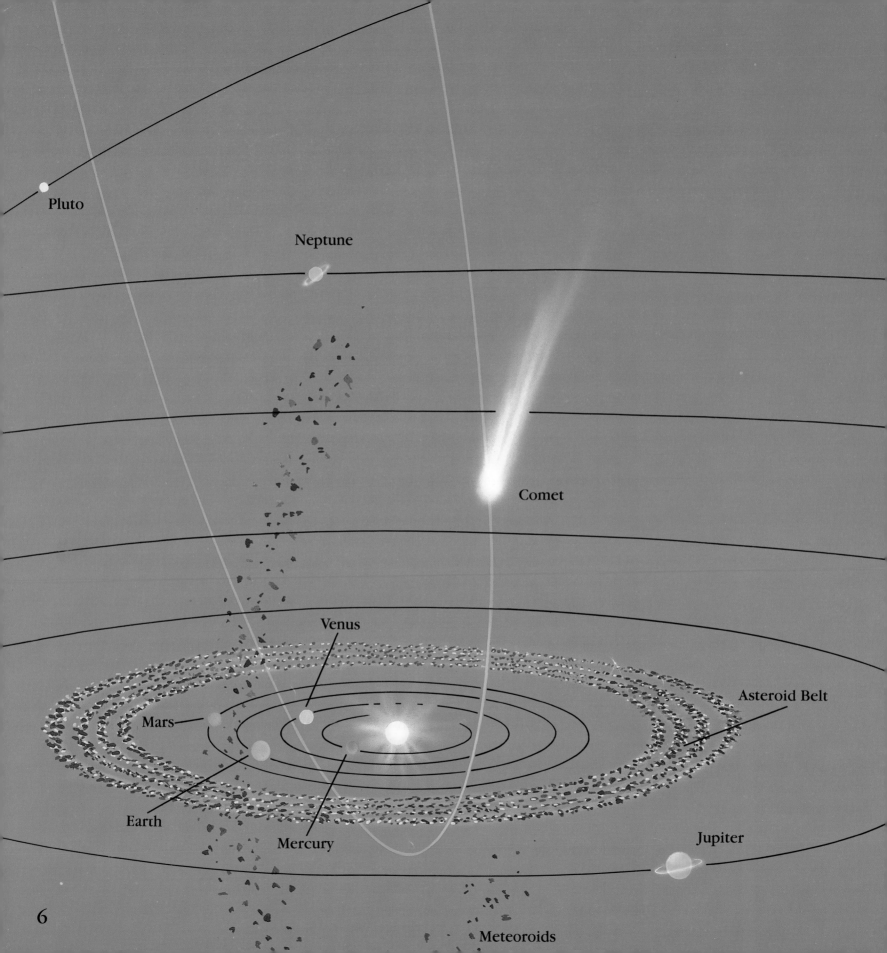

Pluto

Neptune

Comet

Venus

Asteroid Belt

Mars

Earth

Mercury

Jupiter

6

Meteoroids

The sun is just an ordinary star among the more than one hundred billion stars in the galaxy. It is not the biggest or the brightest star. But the sun is the star nearest to our planet, Earth, and the center of the Solar System.

Nine planets travel around the sun in paths called orbits. Mercury, Venus, Earth, and Mars are called the inner planets. These four rocky planets are much smaller than the four giant outer planets—Jupiter, Saturn, Uranus, and Neptune—which are made mostly of gases. Pluto is the smallest and outermost planet. Seven of the planets, including Earth, have moons circling around them.

Thousands of minor planets, called asteroids, also orbit the sun. Many of these lumps of rock circle the sun in a broad "asteroid belt" between the orbits of the planets Mars and Jupiter. Still other, smaller rocks, called meteoroids, as well as many comets, travel around the sun.

Saturn

Uranus

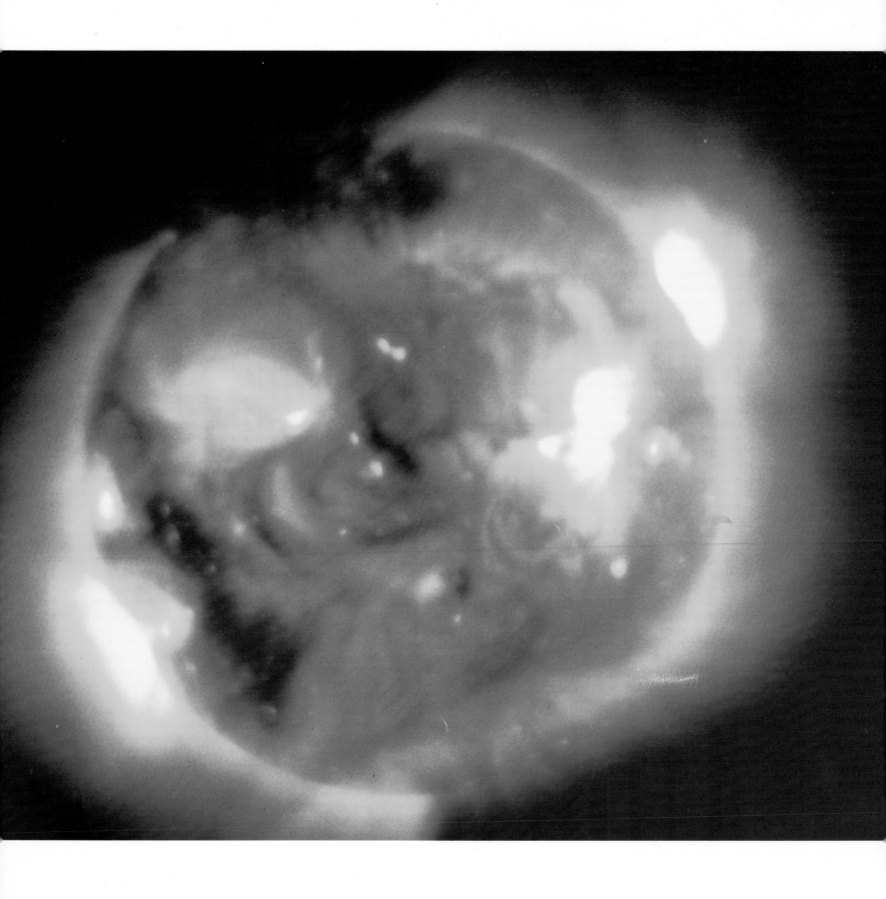

The sun is huge compared to Earth. If the sun were hollow, it could hold 1.3 *million* Earths. Think of this: If Earth were the size of a basketball, the sun would be a giant globe as big as a basketball court. In fact, the sun is about six hundred times bigger than all the planets, moons, asteroids, comets, and meteoroids in the Solar System put together.

Hydrogen is the sun's fuel. Like an endless hydrogen bomb, the sun uses about four million tons of hydrogen every second. Still, the sun has enough hydrogen to continue shining for another five to six billion years.

The sun is all-important to life on Earth. Green plants need sunlight to grow. Animals eat plants for food, and we need animals and plants to live. Our weather and climate depend on the sun. Without the sun, there would be no heat, no light, no clouds, no rain—no living thing on Earth.

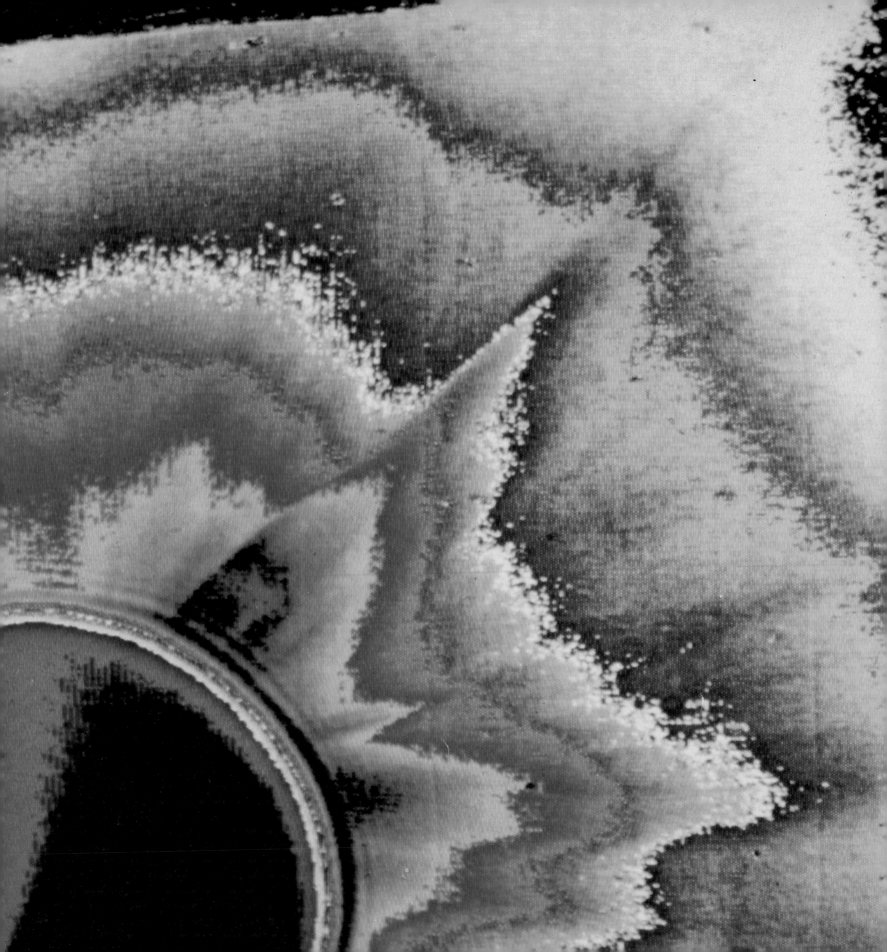

At the very center of the sun is its core, about as big as the planet Jupiter. Here, constant explosions raise the temperature as high as 27 million degrees (F). Surrounding the core are two layers, called the radiative zone and the convective zone.

The sun's surface is called the photosphere, a sea of boiling gases about ten thousand degrees (F). But there are some hotter areas that form, just like bubbles in boiling water.

Giant storms called sunspots also erupt on the surface. Flaming streams of gases called prominences sometimes arch up from sunspots through the sun's atmosphere. Prominences can travel at speeds of two hundred miles per second and stretch for more than one hundred thousand miles.

The sun has an inner atmosphere, called the chromosphere, and an outer atmosphere, called the corona. The corona stretches outward for millions of miles into space. During a total solar eclipse, the corona is visible as a halo around the sun.

Mercury is the closest planet to the sun. It was named by the Romans after the fleet messenger of their gods. Mercury revolves quickly around the sun but rotates very slowly on its axis, so a day on Mercury is almost as long as a year.

Mercury is the second smallest planet in our Solar System, after Pluto. Mercury is much smaller than Earth. In fact, it is smaller than Jupiter's and Saturn's largest moons. Mercury itself has no moons.

Mercury is often hard to spot because it is visible only during twilight hours on some days, close to the sun's bright glare. When Mercury is viewed from Earth through a telescope, it appears to change its shape from day to day, much the way our moon does.

EARTH

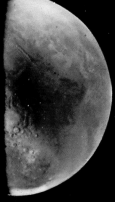

MARS

MERCURY

MOON
(Earth)

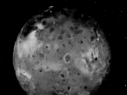

IO
(Jupiter)

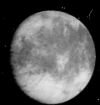

EUROPA
(Jupiter)

GANYMEDE
(Jupiter)

CALLISTO
(Jupiter)

VENUS

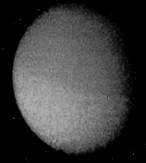

TITAN
(Saturn)

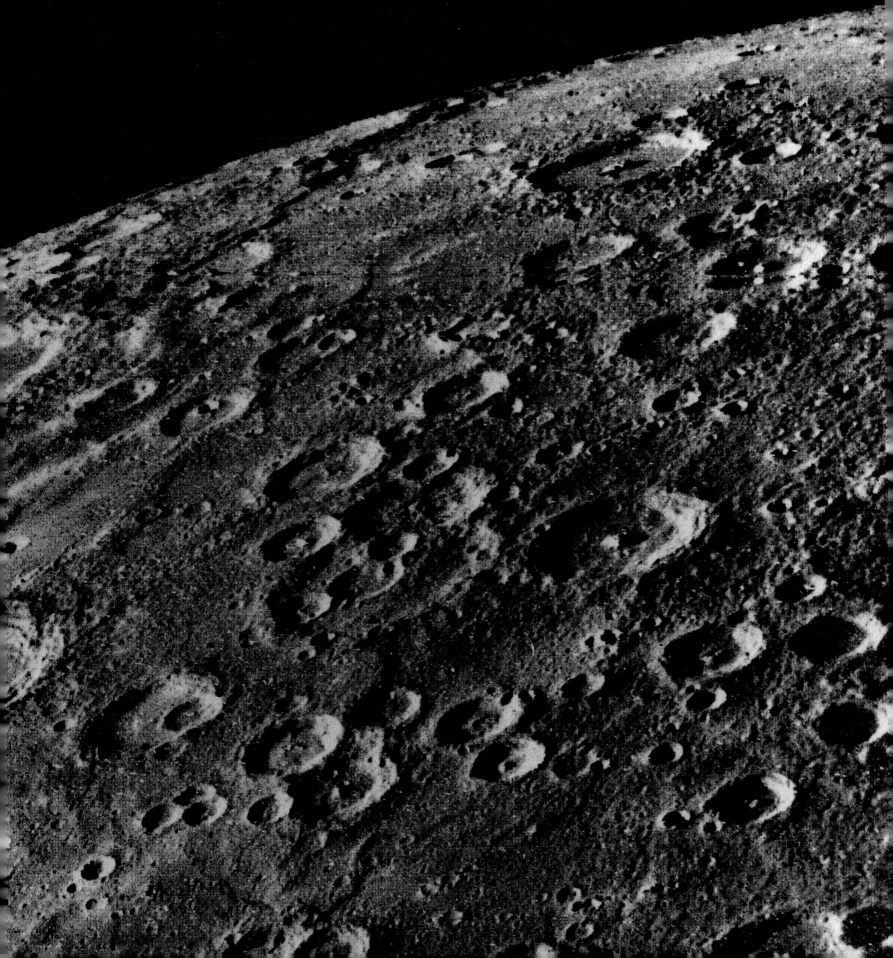

The surface of Mercury is heavily cratered, like that of our moon. The larger craters were made by countless meteorites or asteroids crashing into the surface, which is not protected by an atmosphere. Many smaller craters also spot the terrain. Most of these were made when rocks thrown up from the impact of a meteorite came crashing back down.

Mercury is an almost airless planet. Because Mercury is so close to the sun, the temperature rises above 750 degrees (F) during the day, hot enough to melt lead. Yet during the long nights, with no atmosphere to trap the heat, the temperature on the dark side drops to -300 degrees (F), colder than Earth's South Pole.

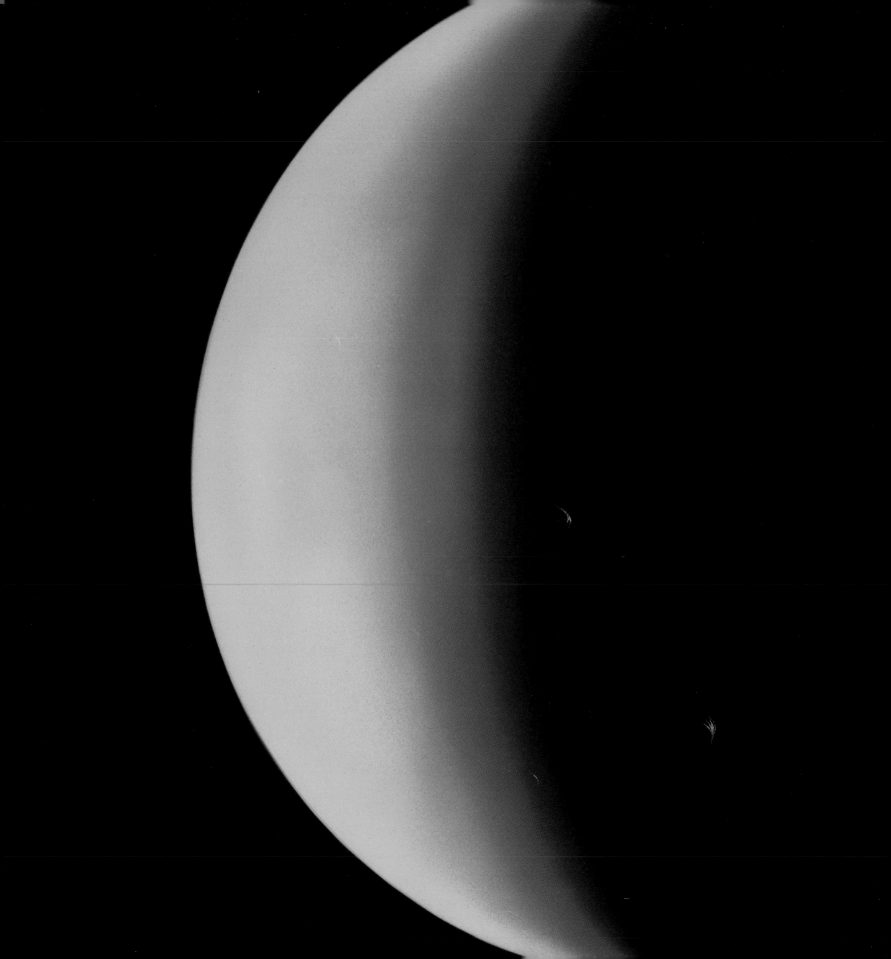

Venus is the brightest object in the night sky after our moon. The Romans named the brilliant planet Venus after their goddess of love and beauty. Venus is sometimes called the Evening Star or the Morning Star. But Venus is not a star. It is the second planet from the sun, after Mercury and just before Earth. Venus rotates from east to west, the opposite of most other planets and moons in the Solar System. Venus is a bit smaller than Earth, and it has no moons.

From Earth, Venus seems to change its shape just as our moon does. When it is close to Earth, Venus appears much larger than when it is on the other side of the sun. But the clouds covering the surface reflect light so well that Venus appears bright even when it is far away.

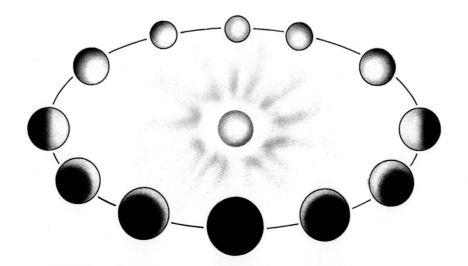

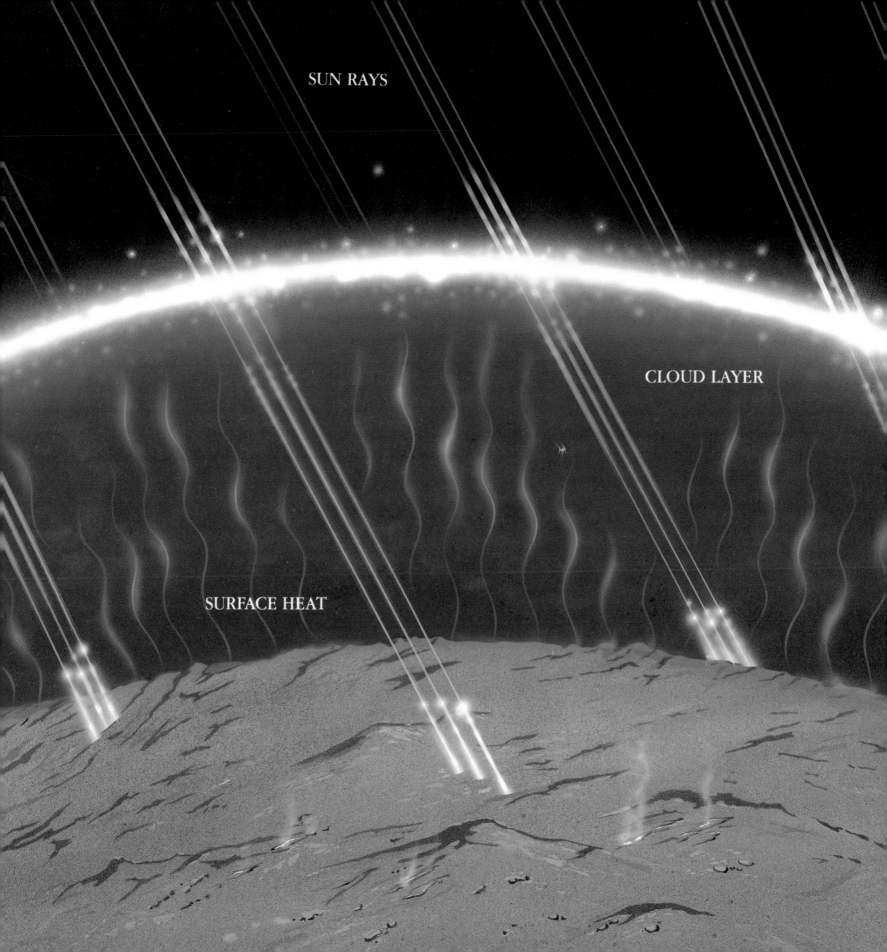

Venus is sometimes called Earth's sister planet because they are about the same size. But Venus is very different from Earth. Like Earth, Venus is covered by thick layers of clouds. But there is very little water on Venus, so the clouds around it are not made of water droplets; instead they are composed of droplets of sulfuric acid. Below the clouds is a thick atmosphere of carbon dioxide.

Venus is a scorching desert, with temperatures of 900 degrees (F), the hottest planet in the Solar System. Venus's atmosphere is mostly responsible for the intense heat. Sunlight passes through the atmosphere and heats the rocky surface. The rocks radiate heat, and the atmosphere traps the heat and doesn't allow it to escape. This is called the greenhouse effect because the glass windows in a greenhouse act in the same way.

NASA's *Magellan* spacecraft has been orbiting and photographing Venus since August 10, 1990. It uses a special kind of radar that shows surface details down to the size of a football field, with ten times the clarity of any previous photos.

This global view of the surface of Venus was computer-produced from the first cycle of *Magellan* mapping. The colors are based on the images taken by the earlier Soviet spacecraft. Venus has large craters but no small ones. That's because the planet's atmosphere is so dense that it stops smaller incoming meteors before they can hit the ground and make a crater.

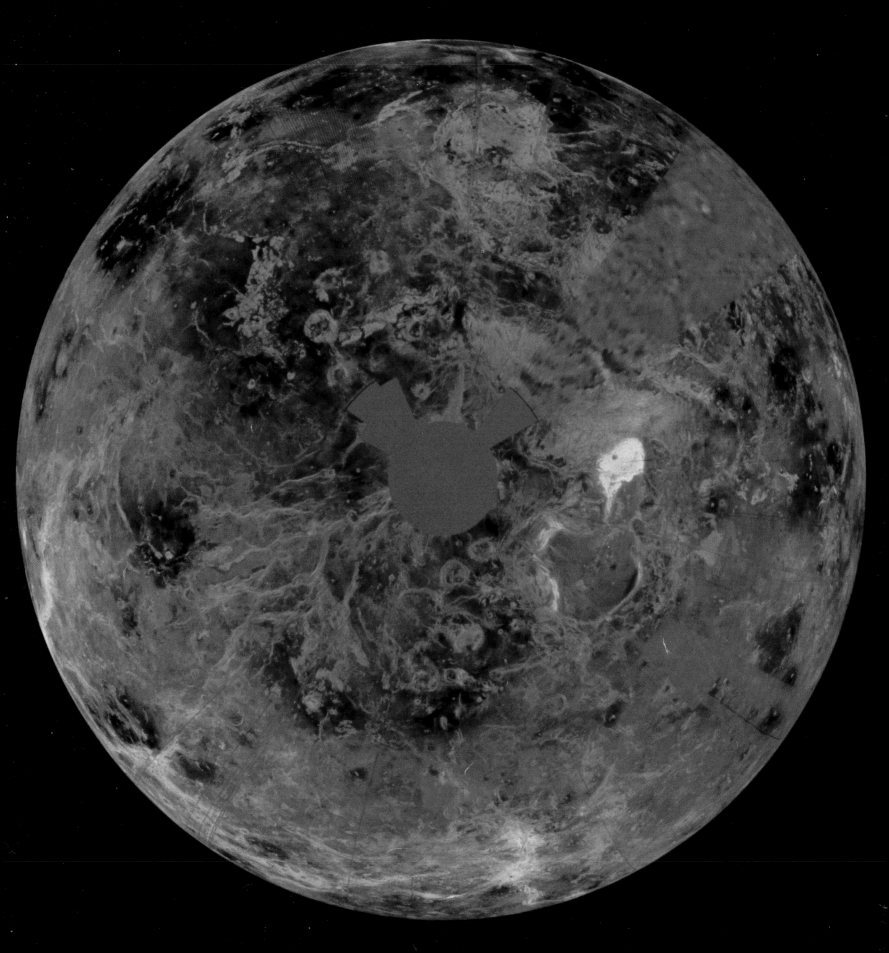

Earth might have been named "Oceans" or "Water." That's because Earth is the only planet in the Solar System with large amounts of liquid water on its surface and in its atmosphere. Earth is the third planet from the sun. If the sun were much closer, the seas would boil away. If the sun were farther away, the water would freeze over. The sun is just the right distance for life to exist on Earth. As far as we know, Earth is the only planet that has living things.

This photograph of Earth from space was taken by the *Apollo 15* astronauts as they headed home from the moon. The brown places are land and the dark blue places are oceans. The white clouds are part of Earth's atmosphere.

Earth is larger than Mercury, Venus, Mars, and Pluto but much smaller than Jupiter, Saturn, Uranus, and Neptune. From space Earth looks like a perfect ball. In fact, Earth is about twenty-seven miles wider at the equator than at the poles. As it orbits the sun, Earth spins like a giant top. One complete spin is called a day.

Earth is tilted a little to one side as it travels around the sun. For part of the year, the northern half of Earth has summer because it is tilted toward the sun and gets more direct rays of sunlight for a longer part of the day. During that time, the southern half is tilted away, so it has winter. As Earth continues to orbit, the southern half is tilted toward the sun and has summer, while the northern half is tilted away and has winter.

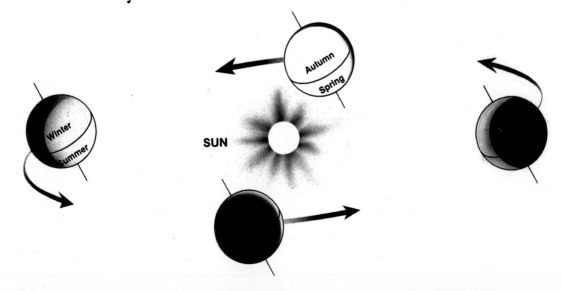

Earth is encircled by a protective blanket of air called the atmosphere, which helps keep the temperature fairly steady. The atmosphere is mostly made up of the gases nitrogen and oxygen, along with a small amount of carbon dioxide and tiny particles of dust and water. We live at the bottom of the atmosphere in a five- to ten-mile layer of air called the troposphere. Most weather takes place in the troposphere. The photo shows the spinning clouds of a typhoon in the troposphere over the Pacific Ocean.

Earth is covered by a five- to thirty-mile-deep layer of rocks called the crust. The solid crust floats on the mantle, an 1,800-mile-thick layer of heavy, melted rock. The crust is cracked into a number of huge pieces called plates. Volcanoes and earthquakes shake the land where the plates meet each other, such as along the rim of the Pacific Ocean.

Earth's crust is constantly changing. This is a photograph of a mountainous area in the western United States. Mountains are pushed up by pressures within the earth. Cracks in the rocks, called faults, run through the crust. The rocks also wear away. Gravel washes down from the tops of mountains into the valleys below. In the winter, ice breaks up rocks. People also change the land. They farm the land and change the course of rivers to provide water. They dig into the land to gather rocks and minerals and use them to build roads and cities.

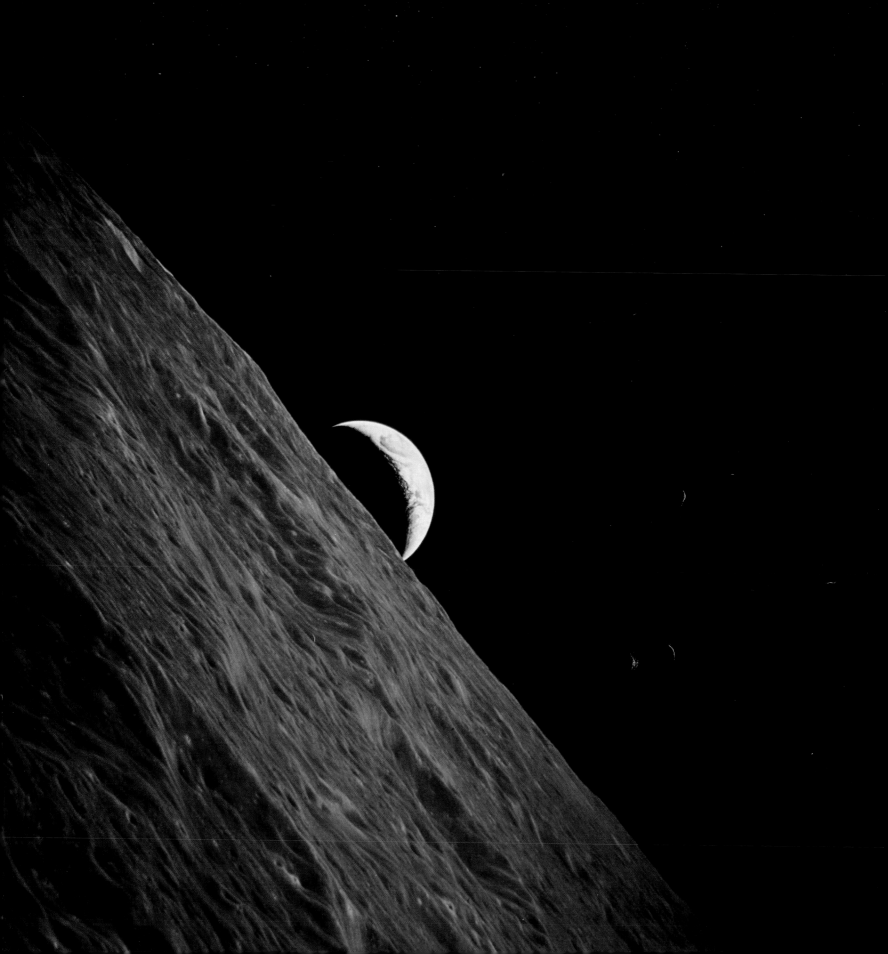

The moon is Earth's closest neighbor in space, only about one-quarter of a million miles away. In space, that is very close. This photo of a crescent Earth over the barren landscape of the moon was taken by the *Apollo 17* astronauts in December 1972.

Earth and the moon are very close to each other in space, but they are very different. Earth is a blue, watery, cloud-covered planet, filled with living things. The moon is a barren place, with no water, no air, no clouds, no living things.

The moon is Earth's only natural satellite. It is about 2,160 miles across, much smaller than Earth. We can see only the part of the moon lit by sunlight. So every night the moon looks a little different. We call the changes in the moon's appearance phases. The phases go from an all-dark new moon, to a sliver called a crescent moon, to a full moon, and back again to a new moon in about twenty-nine days.

The moon's surface is covered by thousands of bowl-shaped craters. The craters were formed by rocky meteorites or asteroids crashing into the moon, which is not protected by an atmosphere. The fifty-mile-wide crater at the top of the photo is called Copernicus, after a famous astronomer who lived long ago. Some craters are even larger, but most are smaller; some are only a few feet wide. The moon's surface is also covered with mountains and hills, valleys and flatlands.

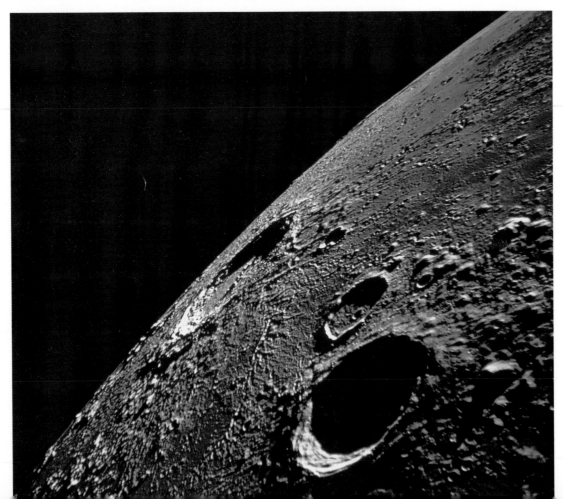

In 1969 and the early 1970s, astronauts from the Apollo space program landed on the moon to gather information. Because the moon's gravity is only one-sixth that of Earth's, the astronauts could easily move about on the moon's surface. The moon is about the same age as Earth, but the astronauts found that the soil and rocks are different. Scientists think that the moon was much hotter a long time ago and that some of the elements on the surface were boiled off into space.

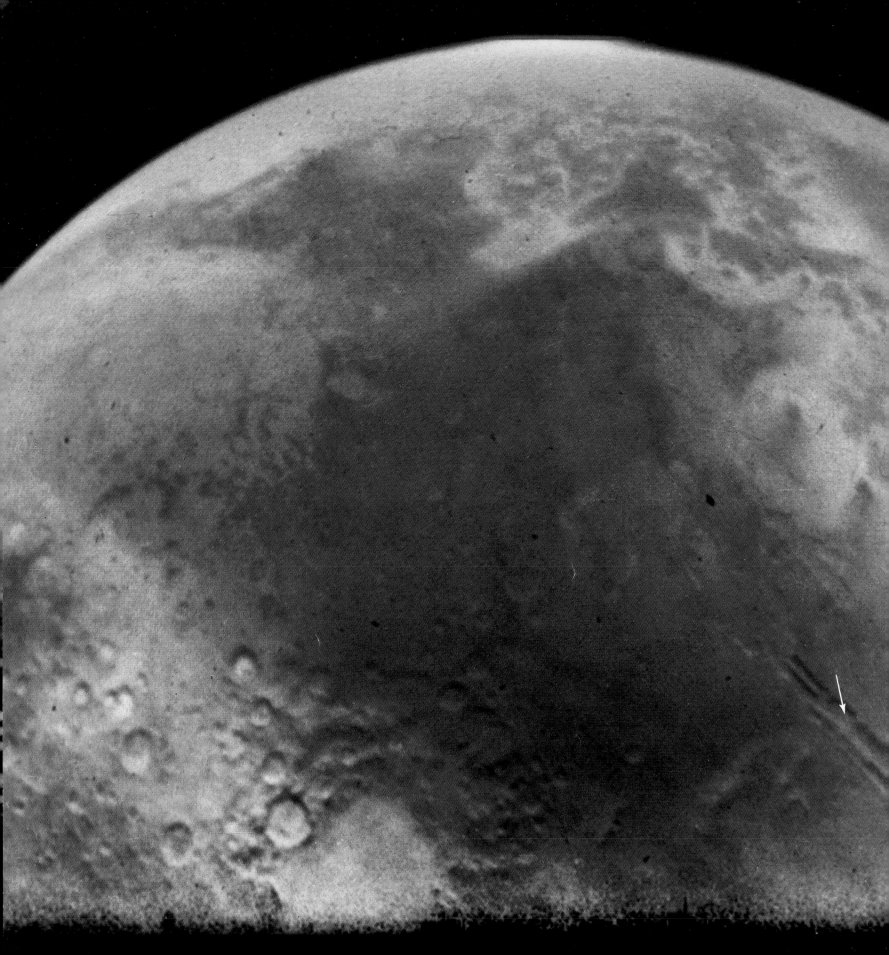

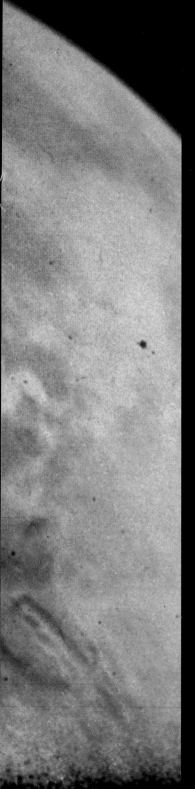

Mars is the fourth planet from the sun. It appears so bright in the night sky because it is closer to us than any other planet except Venus. Because it shines with a red color, it made the early Romans think of blood and war. So they named the planet Mars, after their god of war.

People once imagined that Mars was covered by straight, dark lines. They thought that these lines were giant canals built by intelligent Martians. But in the 1970s, unmanned spacecraft from Earth reached Mars. This view of Mars was sent back from a *Viking* spacecraft. It shows that Mars has craters, mountains, valleys (arrow) deeper and longer than the Grand Canyon—but no canals.

The surface of Mars is covered by orange-red, dusty soil, which is blown from one spot to another by the wind in the very cold, thin atmosphere. The orange-red color is due to the presence of the chemical iron oxide in the soil and rocks. Millions of years ago, when Mars was a young planet, water flowed on the surface. Some water may still remain hidden in underground reservoirs. Even though there is no liquid water on the surface, lots of ice covers the polar caps of Mars. Some of the ice is frozen water, and some is frozen carbon dioxide, also called dry ice.

Is there life on Mars? Two *Viking* landers were supposed to find out. A sample of soil was picked up by a robot arm on each lander and brought into a small computer-controlled biology laboratory on board. Experiments looked for any traces of life in the soil. Scientists are still arguing about the results. Many scientists think that the experiments showed that there is no life on Mars. But other scientists are not so sure. They say that, while we have not discovered life, it may still exist in some unexplored place on the planet.

Jupiter is the giant planet of the Solar System, more than one and a half times as big as all the other planets put together. If Jupiter were hollow, more than 1,300 planet Earths could fit inside. Jupiter is the fifth planet from the sun and was named after the ruler of the Roman gods.

Jupiter is a gas planet of hydrogen and helium, covered by constantly moving clouds hundreds of miles thick. The clouds on Jupiter are not made of water droplets like clouds on Earth, but mostly hydrogen gas.

One of the many mysteries on Jupiter is a giant windstorm called the Great Red Spot. It's nearly three times the size of the whole Earth. The spot was first seen through a telescope more than three hundred years ago. At different times, it has shrunk or grown, turned dull pink or become bright red. But it has not changed position and has kept the same oval shape for centuries.

One of *Voyager's* most exciting discoveries was that Jupiter had a thin ring circling the planet. The photograph shows the edge of Jupiter and part of the ring (right). It was taken in the planet's shadow, after *Voyager* passed by Jupiter on its way to Saturn. All of the four giant outer planets, which are composed mostly of gases, have rings: Jupiter, Saturn, Uranus, and Neptune.

Jupiter is a planet unlike Earth in many ways. The temperature at the cloud tops is very cold—over 250 degrees (F) below freezing. Its surface is an ocean of liquid hydrogen that may be ten thousand or more miles deep. At its center, Jupiter is very hot. The heat from below stirs up the liquid hydrogen and the cloud tops, so that they rise and sink. Life as we know it could not exist on Jupiter. Jupiter and the outer planets are strange and alien places that we have only begun to explore.

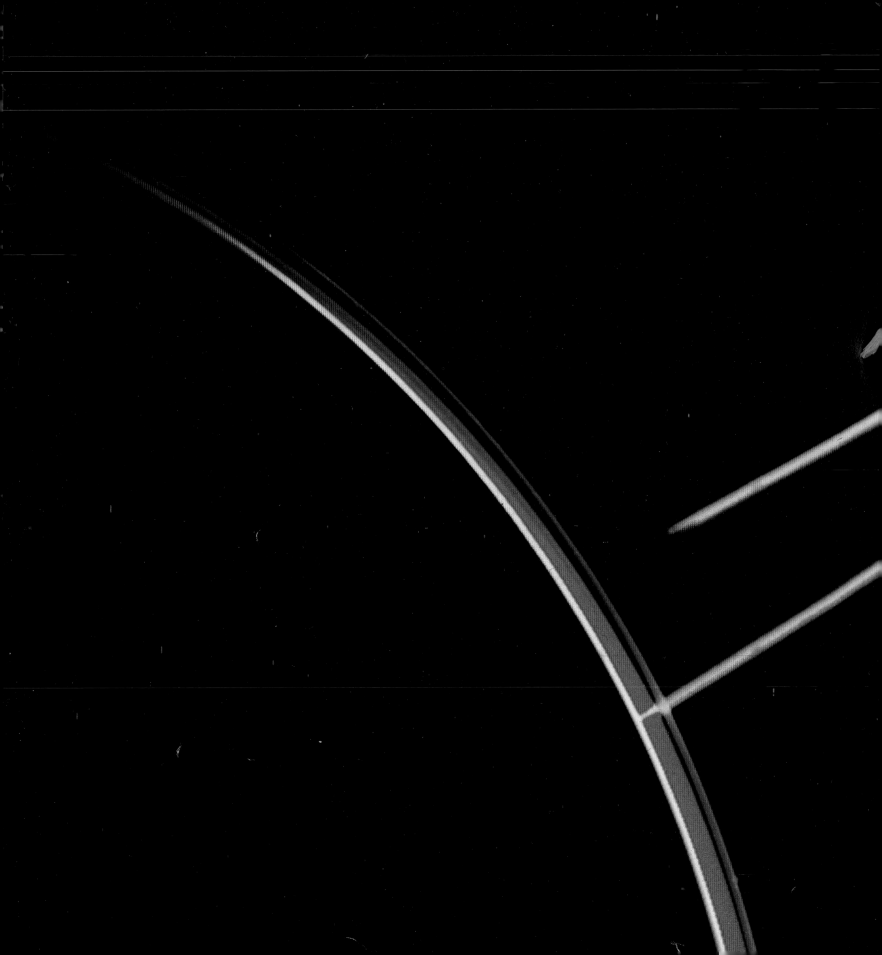

Jupiter has at least sixteen moons. The outer moons are small, most under fifty miles across. The four largest moons are named Io, Europa, Ganymede, and Callisto. These are called the Galilean moons, after Galileo, the great scientist who discovered them in 1610 with his small homemade telescope.

Nearly four hundred years after Galileo, the *Voyager* spaceships gave us close-up looks at the moons of Jupiter. Ganymede is the biggest, larger than the planet Mercury. Europa is covered by a smooth ocean of ice. Callisto is ice with small amounts of rock on top of a deep, frozen ocean.

Io (below) has something that no other moon in the Solar System has: exploding volcanoes. The volcanoes often erupt, sending out flows of hot liquid sulfur. The surface of Io changes with each new eruption. The sulfur changes color as it cools. The black spot in the lower part of the photo is the crater of a dead volcano.

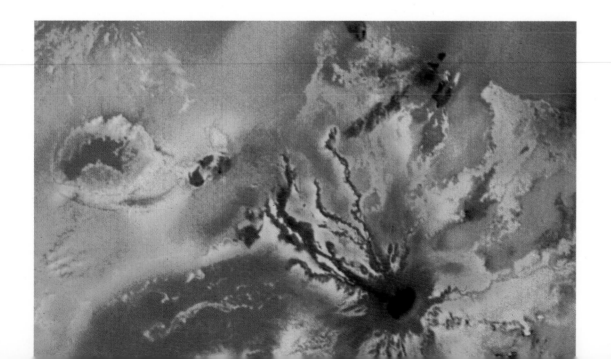

Saturn is the second-largest planet, after Jupiter. If Saturn were hollow, about 750 planet Earths could fit inside. Like Jupiter, Saturn is a gas planet, made up mostly of hydrogen and helium. Saturn is the sixth planet from the sun and was named after the Roman god of farming.

The great scientist Galileo looked at Saturn through his low-power telescope nearly four centuries ago. He was shocked to see what looked like ears on either side of the planet. Galileo decided that they were two smaller globes on either side of Saturn. About fifty years later, an astronomer with a stronger telescope saw that the two globes were really a flat ring around the planet.

Even if you look through a powerful telescope on Earth, Saturn appears to have just a few rings. But the *Voyager* spacecraft took photos that show that the large rings are made of thousands of smaller rings within rings. There are so many rings around Saturn, they look like the grooves in a phonograph record.

If you were to get even closer, you would see that the rings are made of pieces of ice. Some are as small as a fingernail; others, as big as a house. The rings also contain dust and bits of rock. And all of the materials in the rings spin around Saturn like millions of tiny moons.

The rings are nearly 170 thousand miles across but are less than three miles thick, and some are even thinner. How did the rings form? Some scientists think that the rings around the gas planets contain materials left over when the planets formed. Perhaps pieces of nearby moons that were chipped off by incoming meteorites help to form rings. No one knows for sure.

Saturn has the most moons of any planet in the Solar System. More than twenty have been discovered, and there are probably others. Saturn has one large moon, six that are medium-sized, and at least fourteen smaller ones. Most of Saturn's moons are ice-covered and pockmarked with craters.

This picture of Saturn and some of its moons was made from a number of photographs taken by *Voyager*. Saturn is partly hidden by Dione. Enceladus and Rhea are off in the distance to the upper left. Tethys and Mimas are off to the lower right. Titan, Saturn's largest moon, is far away at the top right. Titan is bigger than the planets Mercury and Pluto.

Titan is the only moon in the Solar System known to have an atmosphere. The atmosphere is mostly nitrogen gas and covers the moon's surface with a thick haze.

Uranus is the seventh planet from the sun. Years after its discovery by William Herschel through a telescope in 1781, the planet was named Uranus, after the Greek god of heaven and ruler of the world. Uranus is a ringed planet made up mostly of gases, about halfway in size between Jupiter and Earth. If Uranus were hollow, about fifty planet Earths could fit inside.

In January 1986, eight and a half years after it had been launched from Earth, the *Voyager 2* spacecraft swept past the pale blue-green clouds of Uranus. This photograph of Uranus was taken when *Voyager* was still five million miles from the planet.

Uranus is "lying on its side" in space. At the moment, the south end of the axis around which the planet rotates is pointing at the sun. Therefore, the south pole is in the midst of forty-two years of constant sunlight, while the north pole is having a forty-two-year night. Gradually the north pole will point at the sun, and it will have forty-two years of sunlight, while the south pole will be dark.

Uranus has five large moons and at least ten smaller ones. This view shows part of Miranda, innermost of the five larger moons, circling only sixty-five thousand miles away from the cloud tops of ringed Uranus. Miranda is the strangest of the moons. Huge canyons, deep grooves, ridges, and ropelike markings cover its surface—all this on a moon only three hundred miles across.

Uranus has eleven thin rings, along with parts of other rings. The rings are made of chunks of an unknown black material spinning around Uranus like lumps of coal on a merry-go-round.

Neptune is too far from Earth to be seen without a telescope. Galileo saw Neptune through his small telescope but mistook it for a star. It was first identified as a planet in 1846. Later the planet was named Neptune, after the Roman god of the sea. Neptune is just a bit smaller than Uranus.

Neptune is a ringed gas planet with dark storms, giant hurricanes, and streaky white clouds of methane-ice that float thirty-five miles above the lower cloud deck. The largest storm is big enough to swallow our entire planet Earth. Strong, frigid winds in the atmosphere blow at the fastest speeds ever measured on a planet, up to seven hundred miles per hour. Methane in the atmosphere absorbs red light, which is the reason for the planet's blue color. Haze high above the clouds causes the red rim.

Twelve years and more than 2.8 billion miles after leaving Earth, *Voyager 2* whizzed past Neptune on August 25, 1989, and headed on its way out of the Solar System. The spacecraft found that Neptune has two bright outer rings, a fainter inner ring, and a thin ring of dusty material. Scientists will need years to examine and understand all the information *Voyager* has provided about the outer planets.

"A world unlike any other" is how scientists described Neptune's moon Triton. Neptune has at least two large moons and six smaller ones. Triton is the biggest, about 1,700 miles across, nearly the same size as our own moon. Triton is colder than any other object ever measured in the Solar System. Large parts of its surface look like the rind of an orange, with gigantic cracks across the surface. Triton was once a hot, volcanic place, but now it is "the frozen imprint of that earlier era."

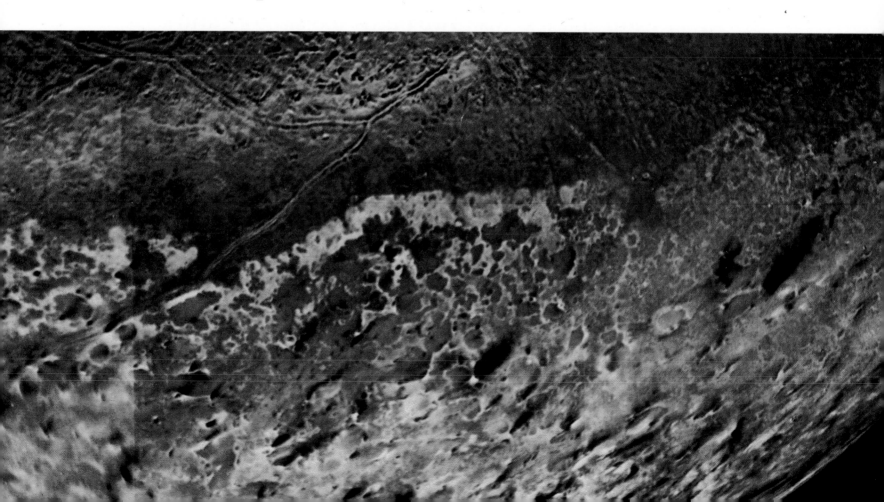

Pluto is the ninth planet of the Solar System and usually the most distant. But Pluto has an odd, stretched and tilted orbit, which brings it closer to the sun than Neptune for 20 out of every 250 years. So, between 1979 and 1999, Pluto is closer to the sun than Neptune.

Pluto was discovered by Clyde Tombaugh, a young American astronomer, in February 1930. The planet remained undiscovered for many years because it is so far from Earth and less than two-thirds the size of Earth's moon. Pluto was named after the Greek and Roman god of the underworld.

The smallest and coldest planet in the Solar System, Pluto appears to be an ice ball of methane and water mixed with rock, surrounded by a thin atmosphere of methane gas. Scientists are still not sure whether Pluto is a Neptunian moon knocked out of orbit long ago or an asteroid that strayed into a distant orbit around the sun.

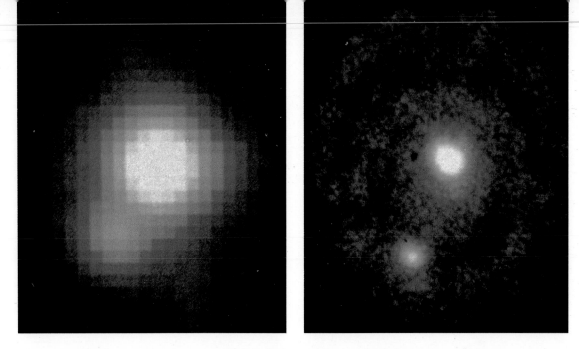

In 1978, astronomers discovered that tiny Pluto has a large moon of its own and named it Charon, after the boatman on the river Styx in the underworld, which Pluto rules. Charon has a diameter almost 40 percent of Pluto's. The moon is so large compared to the planet it circles that Pluto and Charon are often called a double planet. Charon revolves close to Pluto and speeds through its orbit in only about six days and nine hours.

This photo of Pluto and Charon (upper right) was taken by the Hubble Space Telescope in 1990. The best ground-based image of the two (upper left) was taken with the Canada-France-Hawaii telescope in Hawaii.

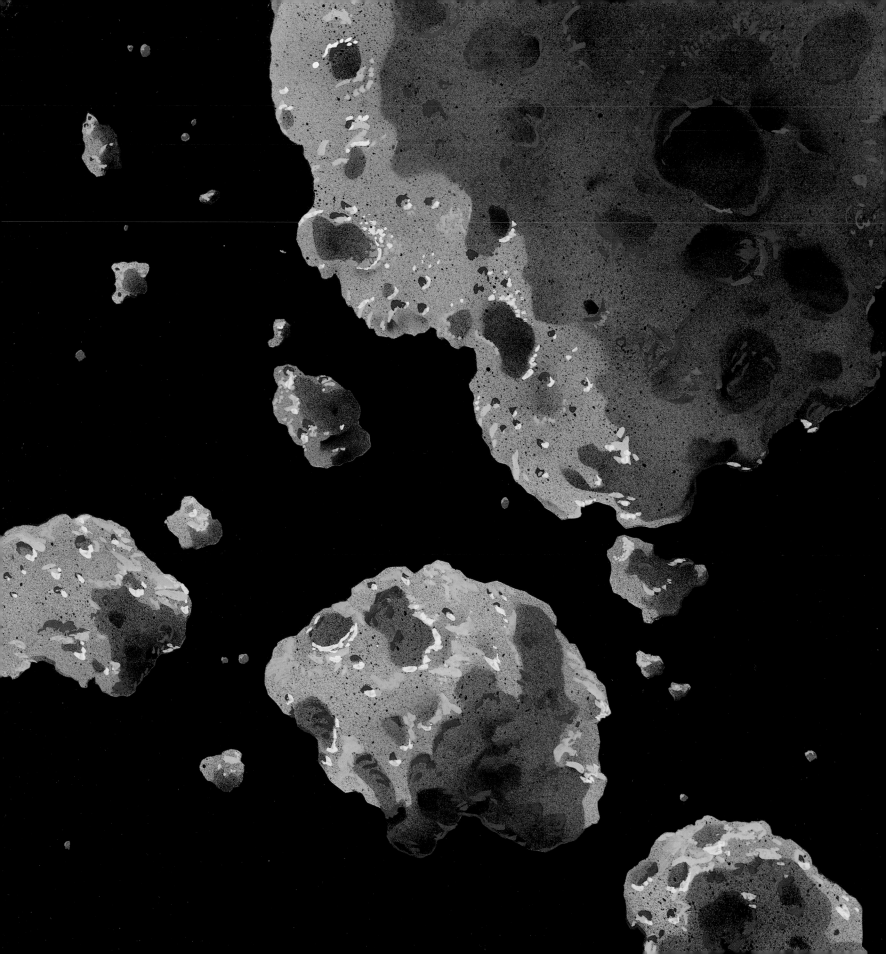

Asteroids are very small worlds that circle the sun, mainly between the orbits of Mars and Jupiter, a region called the asteroid belt. About three thousand asteroids have been discovered, but scientists think that there are many thousands more.

Sometimes called minor planets, all the asteroids combined would not make a world as large as our moon. Most are only a few miles across. Ceres, about six hundred miles in diameter, is by far the largest asteroid. Only Pallas and Vesta are more than three hundred miles in diameter.

Apollo asteroids are a small group that swings in close to the sun and may approach Earth. In 1937, a small asteroid, Hermes, came within a million miles of Earth. That's a close brush in space. Will an asteroid ever hit Earth, and what would happen if it did? Some scientists think that asteroids (or comets) have hit our planet in the past and may hit it in the future. They say that one such impact resulted in the extinction of the dinosaurs.

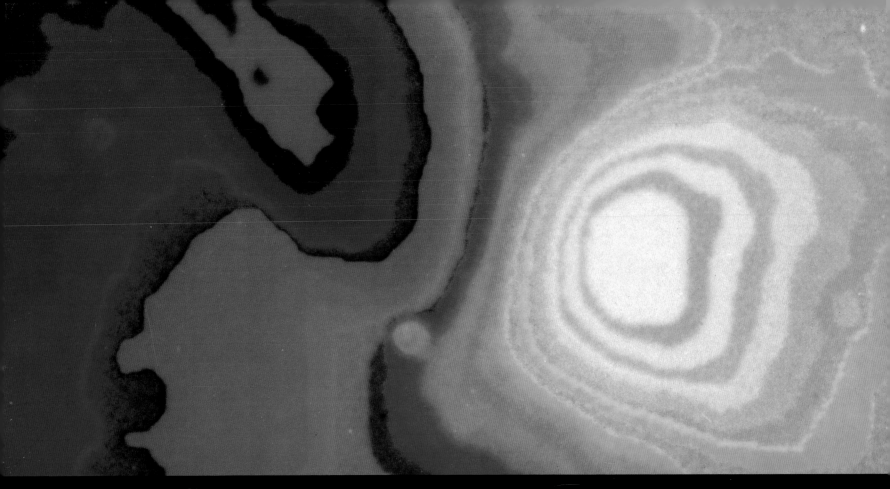

Comets orbit the sun, but they are quite unlike planets. When a comet approaches Earth, it may look spectacular, with a long, glowing tail stretching far across the sky. But comets don't always look like that. Most comets circle the dark edges of the Solar System. Far from the sun, a comet is just a "dirty snowball," a frozen ball of ice a few miles wide, covered by a layer of black dust. This small, dark body is the comet's nucleus.

When a comet sweeps in toward the sun, it begins to

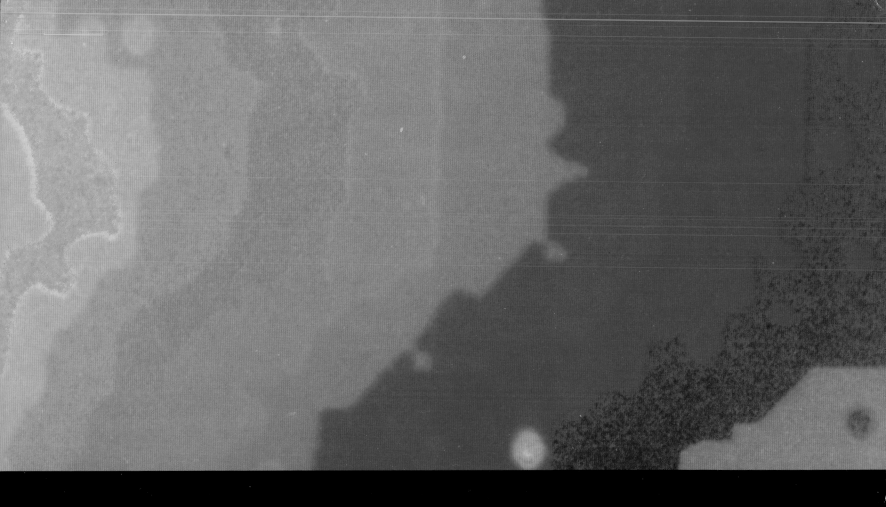

change. The pressure of sunlight and streams of particles from the sun sweep dust off the comet's surface and evaporate some of the ice. The dust and gas begin to glow and form first a halo, called the coma, and then finally a tail, which may stretch millions of miles.

This 1986 photo of Halley's comet was taken from the *Giotto* spacecraft. The nucleus, only twelve thousand miles away, is the dark spot at the upper left. The bright area in the center is a dust jet lit up by sunlight.

Meteoroids are small pieces of metal or rock that may have been swept off asteroids or comets. We can't see them in space, but when a meteoroid enters Earth's atmosphere, we see a bright streak of light flashing across the sky. They are then called meteors. A few of the larger ones may fall to the surface as meteorites. Your chances of being hit by a meteorite are not very great, much less than your chances of being struck by lightning.

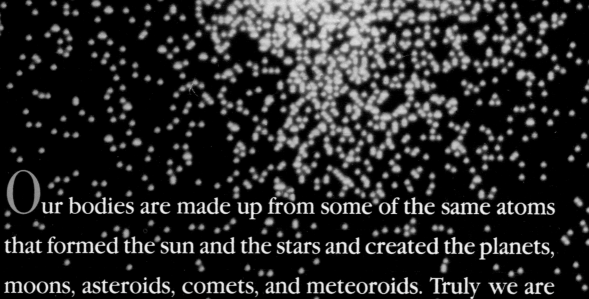

Our bodies are made up from some of the same atoms
that formed the sun and the stars and created the planets,
moons, asteroids, comets, and meteoroids. Truly we are
all children of the universe.

Index

PLANETS OF THE SOLAR SYSTEM

	MERCURY	VENUS	EARTH	MARS
Average distance from sun in miles and kilometers	36 million miles/ 58 million km	67 million miles/ 108 million km	93 million miles/ 150 million km	141 million miles/ 228 million km
Revolution in earth-days, earth-years	88 days	224.7 days	365.26 days	687 days
Rotation in earth-days, hours, minutes	58.6 days	243 days	23 hours, 56 min, 4 sec	24 hours, 37 min, 23 sec
Equatorial diameter in miles	3,031	7,519	7,926.6	4,221
Atmosphere: main gases	almost none	carbon dioxide	nitrogen, oxygen	carbon dioxide
Surface gravity (Earth = 1)	0.38	0.91	1	0.38
Number of known satellites	0	0	1	2
Rings	0	0	0	0

JUPITER

EARTH

MARS

VENUS

MERCURY

SUNSPOTS

SUN